Book, words and music by RUPERT HOLMES

T0055331

CONTENTS

ISBN 978-0-634-08371-6

7777 W. BLUEMOUND RD. P.O. BOX 13819 MILWAUKEE, WI 53213

In Australia Contact:
Hal Leonard Australia Pty. Ltd.
22 Taunton Drive P.O. Box 5130
Cheltenham East, 3192 Victoria, Australia
Email: ausadmin@halleonard.com

Cover illustration by Paul Davis © 1985

Visit Hal Leonard Online at
www.halleonard.com

RUPERT HOLMES

For his Broadway musical **The Mystery of Edwin Drood**, Rupert Holmes became the first person in theatrical history to singly receive Tony Awards for Best Book and Best Music and Lyrics, while **Drood** itself won the Tony Award for Best Musical. The New York Drama Desk bestowed the identical honors to Holmes and his work, with a further award to him in their additional category of Best Orchestration. For his Broadway hit **Say Goodnight, Gracie**, he received another Tony nomination and won the National Broadway Theatre Award for Best Play 2004. The Mystery Writers of America gave Holmes their coveted Edgar Award for his Broadway comedy-thriller **Accomplice**, the second time Holmes has received their highest honor. His *tour de force* for actor Stacy Keach, **Solitary Confinement**, enjoyed a Broadway run and set a new box office mark at The Kennedy Center. Holmes also created and wrote the critically acclaimed, Emmy Award-winning TV series **Remember WENN**, as well as composing its theme and musical underscore. His first novel, **Where the Truth Lies**, received national rave reviews and is soon to be a major motion picture, directed by Atom Egoyan and starring Kevin Bacon and Colin Firth. His second novel, **Swing**, will be published by Random House in March of 2005 with an accompanying CD featuring the book's original big band musical score, arranged and composed by Holmes. For more, visit www.RupertHolmes.com.

The Mystery of Edwin Drood is forever dedicated to
Wendy Isobel Holmes
(1976 – 1986)

THERE YOU ARE

Words and Music by
RUPERT HOLMES

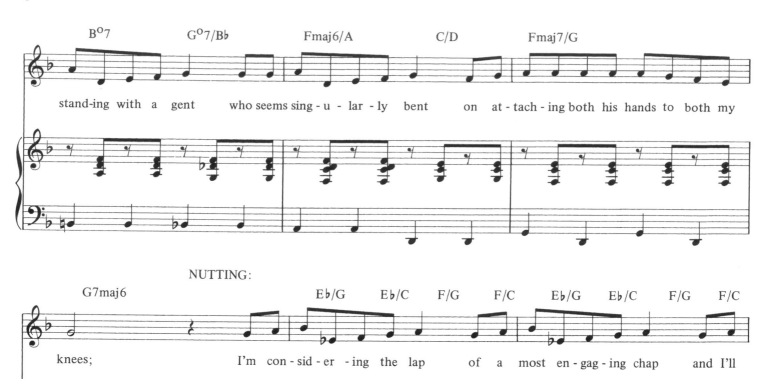

standing with a gent who seems sing-u-lar-ly bent on at-tach-ing both his hands to both my

NUTTING:

knees; I'm con-sid-er-ing the lap of a most en-gag-ing chap and I'll

PAGET:

let him do ex-act-ly as I please. I've a la-dy down in front who's hand-ed

PEREGRINE:

me her latch key. Sure-ly she must know that spells her doom; and this

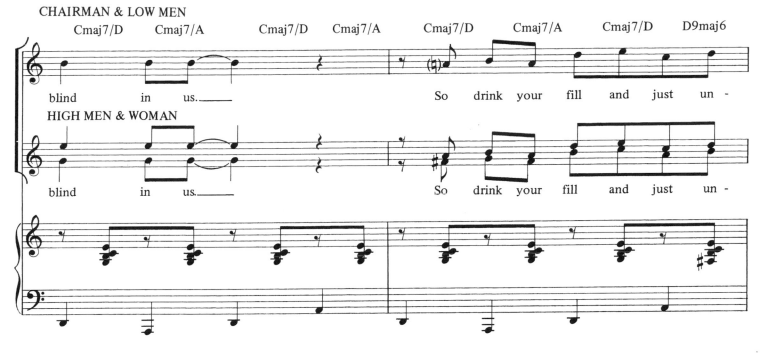

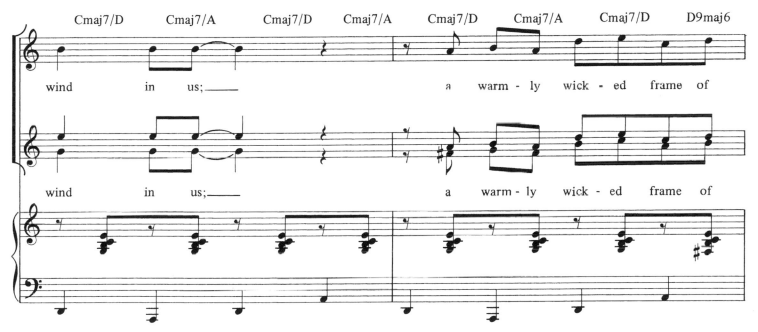

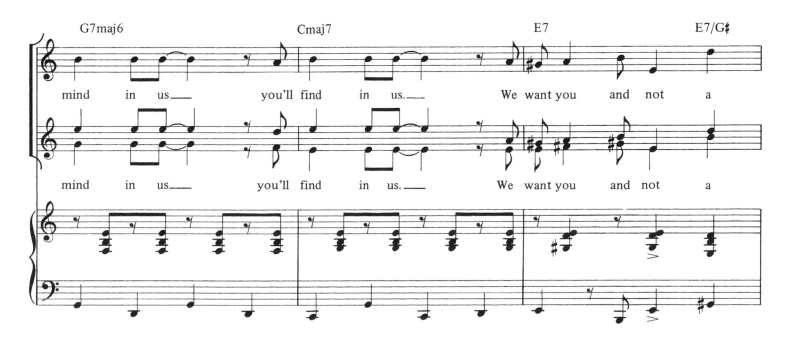

CHAIRMAN & LOW MEN

A MAN COULD GO QUITE MAD

Words and Music by
RUPERT HOLMES

TWO KINSMEN

Words and Music by
RUPERT HOLMES

15

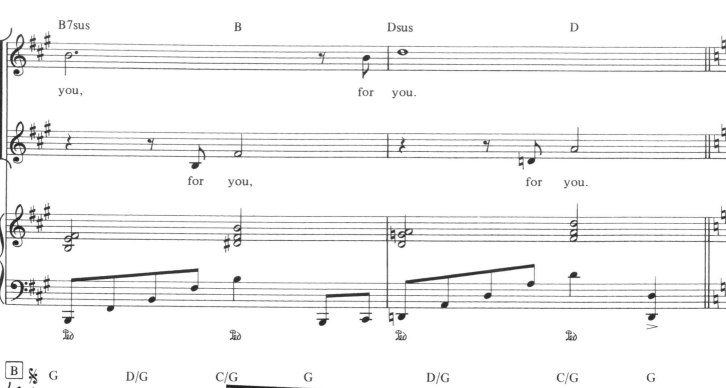

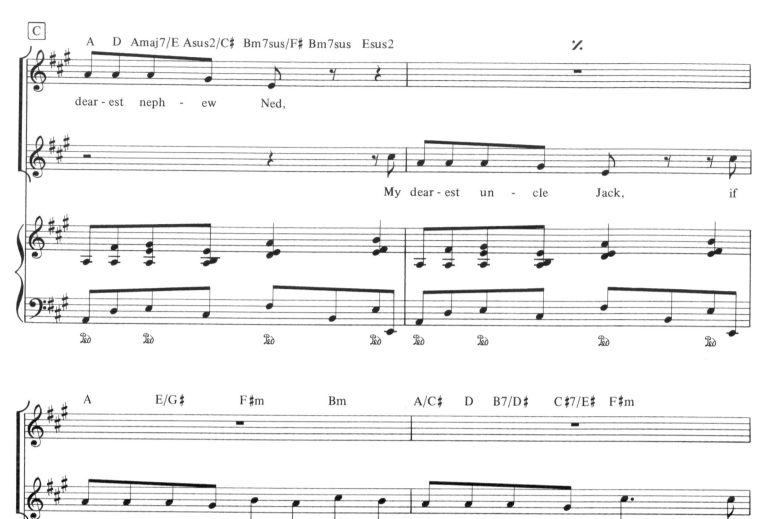

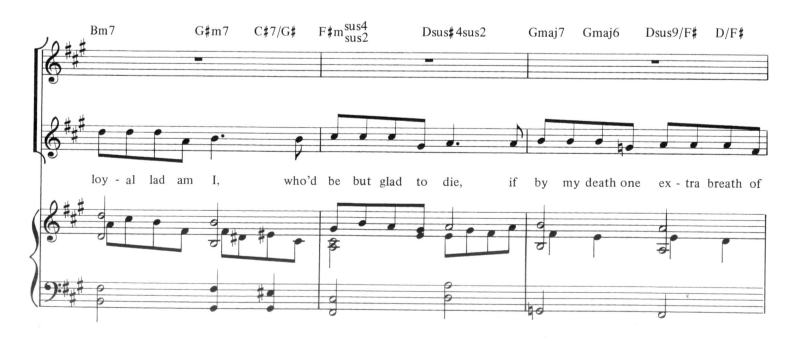

MOONFALL

Words and Music by
RUPERT HOLMES

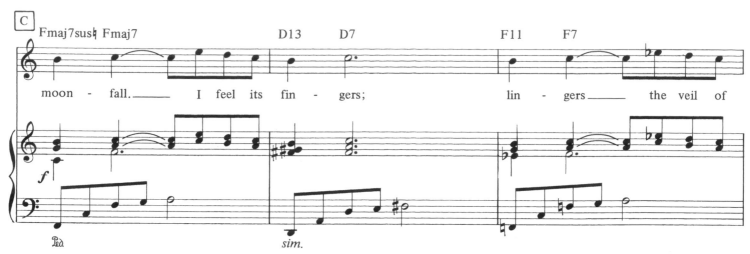

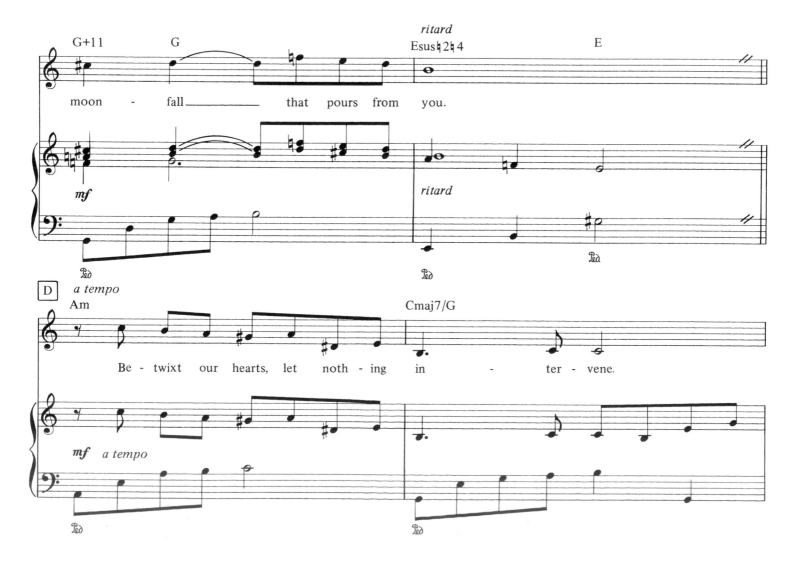

Be - tween our eyes, the on - ly sight I've seen

is lus - trous moon - fall as it blinds my view,

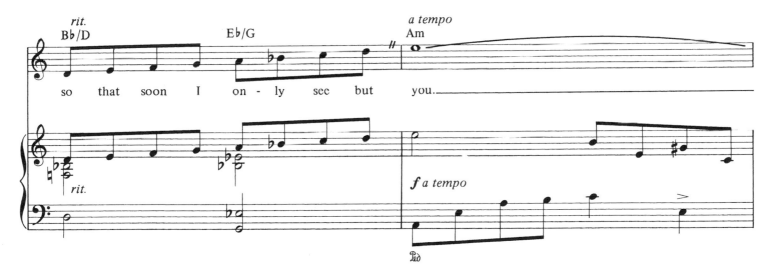

so that soon I on - ly see but you.

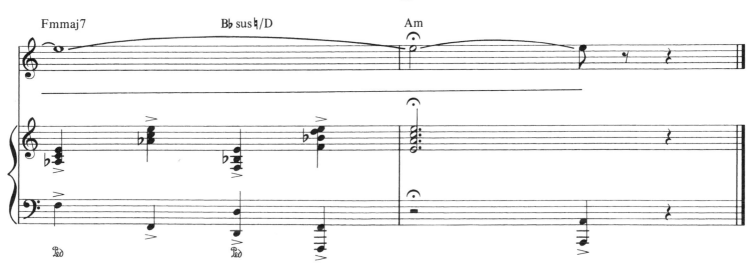

THE WAGES OF SIN

Words and Music by
RUPERT HOLMES

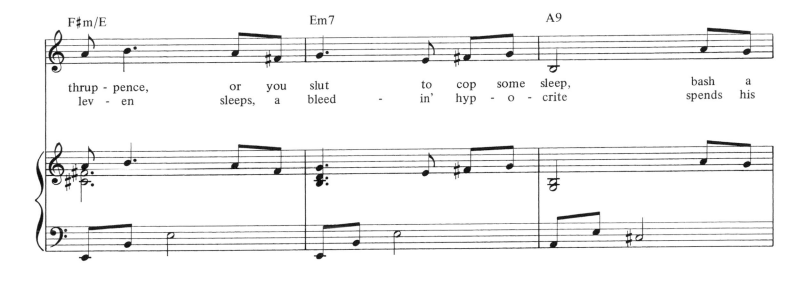

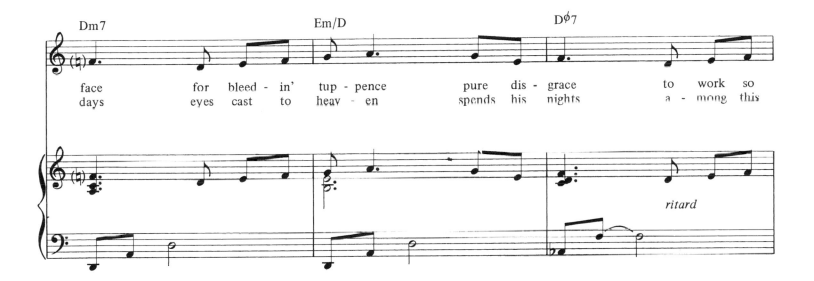

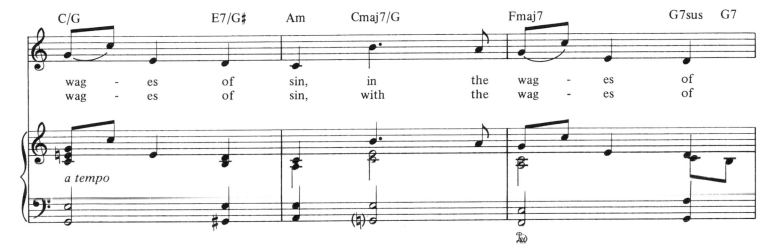

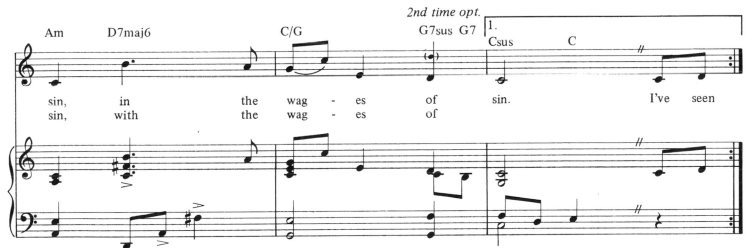

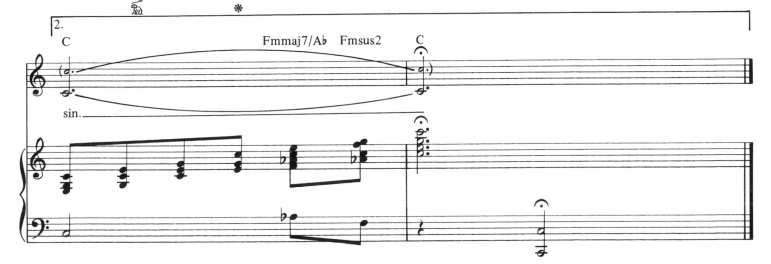

BOTH SIDES OF THE COIN

Words and Music by
RUPERT HOLMES

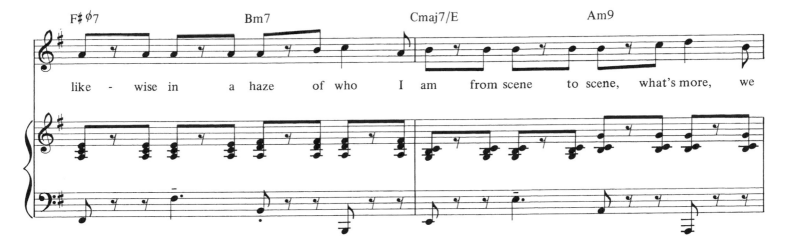

like - wise in a haze of who I am from scene to scene, what's more, we

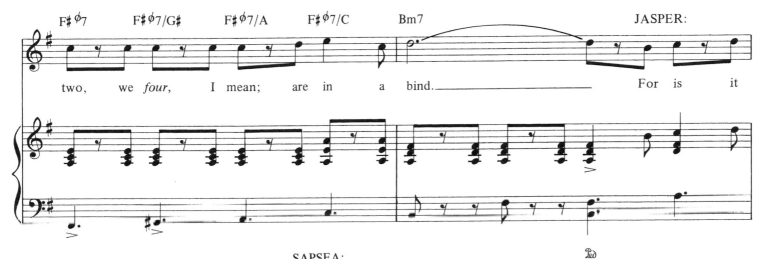

two, we *four*, I mean; are in a bind._____ For is it

JASPER:

SAPSEA:

I or is it me? And if I'm him *and* if I'm he, each one of

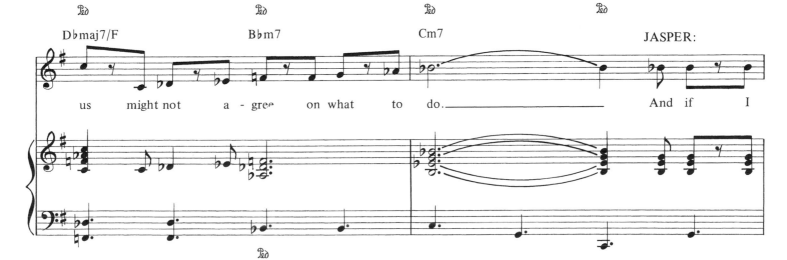

us might not a - gree on what to do._____ And if I

JASPER:

B7/F♯ B7 B7/F♯ B7 Am9/E Am9 Am9/E Am9

would you not fan - cy the cur - ren - cy for - eign to find the same face on both sides of the coin?

ff

B7/F♯ B7 B7/F♯ B7 Cmaj7/G Cmaj7 Cmaj7/G Cmaj7

Bob is your un - cle from pen - nies to guin - eas, the two sid - ed mint is the rule, not ex - cep - tion, and

B7/F♯ B7 B7/F♯ B7 Am9 B7 Em

would you not feel quite the fool of de - cep - tion to find the same face on both sides of the coin?

JASPER:
B7/F♯ B7 B7/F♯ B7 Cmaj7/G Cmaj7 Cmaj7/G Cmaj7

Ha' pen - ny, one pen - ny, tu - pen - ny, thru - pen - ny, twelve to a shil - ling twice that to a flo - rin, and

SAPSEA:
Ah, _____ lah dat da - dah - dah, _____

PERFECT STRANGERS

Words and Music by
RUPERT HOLMES

Too much we've seen to-geth-er_____ to judge the view;

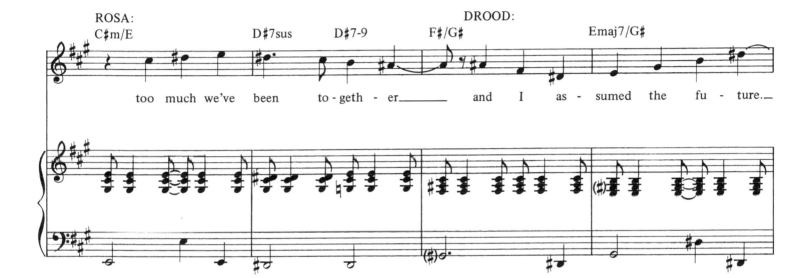

ROSA: too much we've been to-geth-er_____ DROOD: and I as-sumed the fu-ture.___

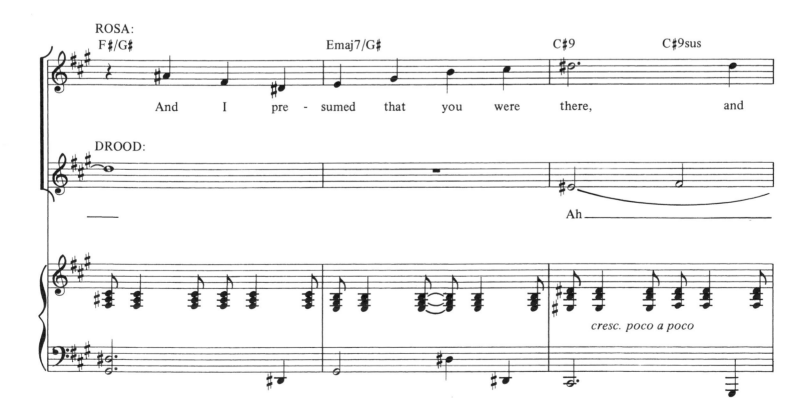

ROSA: And I pre-sumed that you were there, and

DROOD: ___ Ah_____

cresc. poco a poco

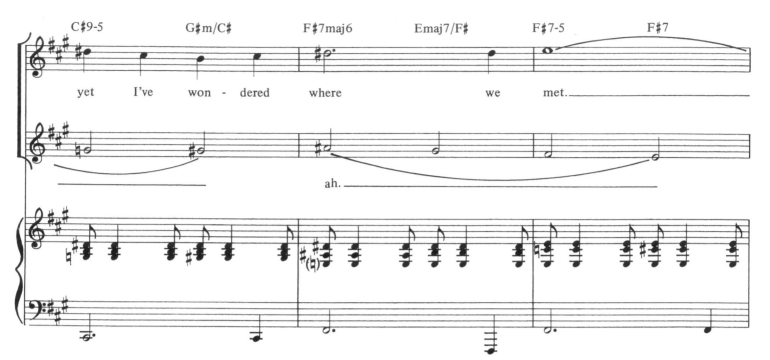

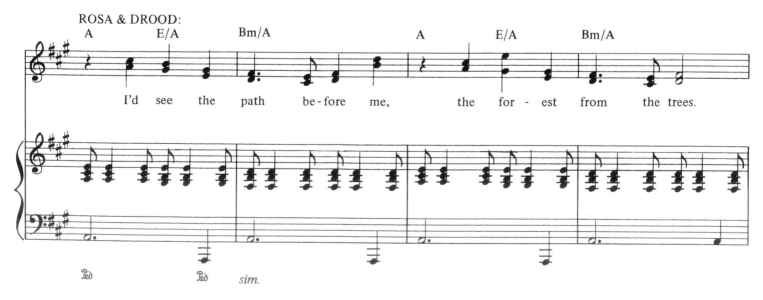

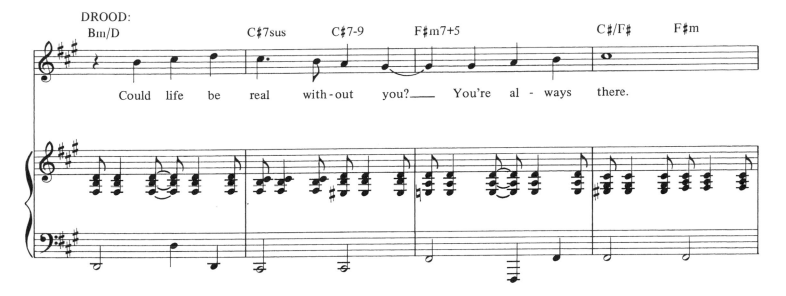

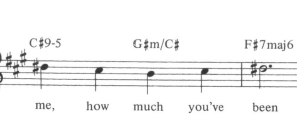

C#9-5　　G#m/C#　　F#7maj6　　Emaj7/F#　　F#7-5　　F#7

me,　how　much　you've　been　to　me.

How would　we know　it?　How could　we feel　it?　How would　we show　it?

ROSA & DROOD:

Bb/F　　F　　Eb/F　　Bb/F　　F　　Eb/F　　F#°7

If　we'd　been　per - fect strang - ers,　I　might　have　loved　you per - fect-

Gm/D　　Gb7/Db　　Am/C　　Db/Cb

ly. _____　Ah. _____

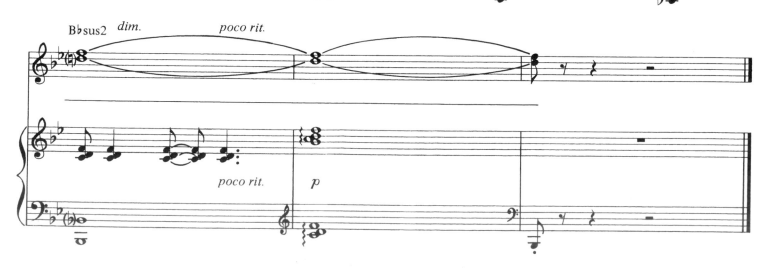

Bbsus2　*dim.*　*poco rit.*

a tempo

poco rit.　*p*

NEVER THE LUCK

Words and Music by
RUPERT HOLMES

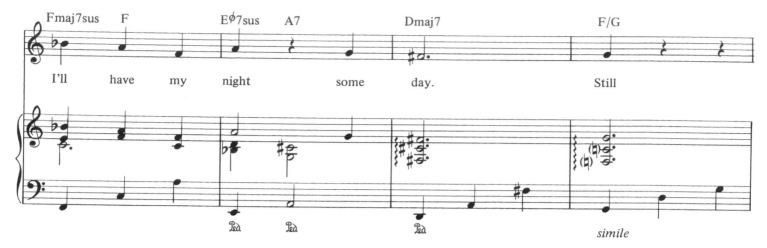

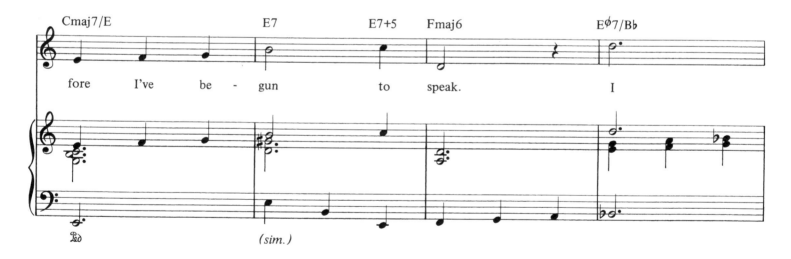

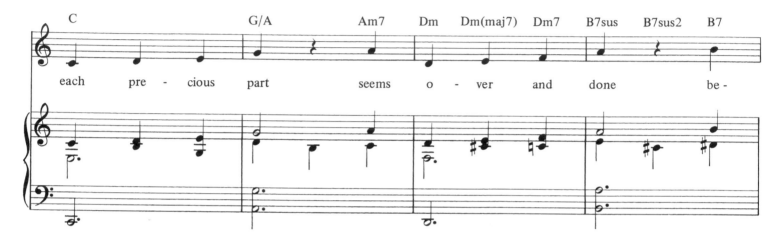

43

waltz my way in - to your heart.

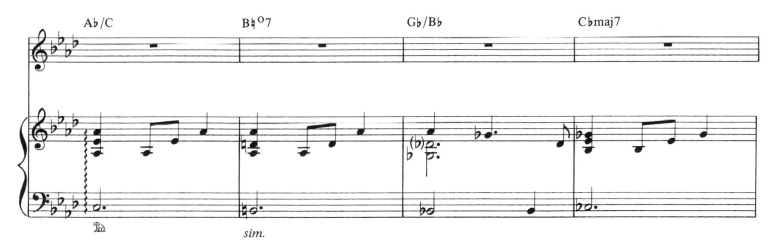

OFF TO THE RACES

Words and Music by
RUPERT HOLMES

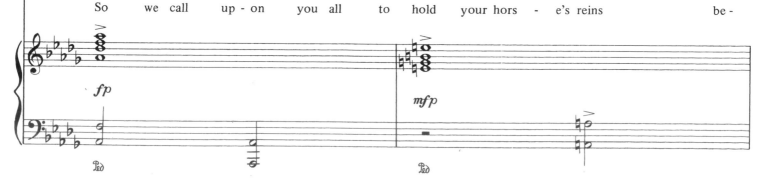

DON'T QUIT WHILE YOU'RE AHEAD

Words and Music by
RUPERT HOLMES

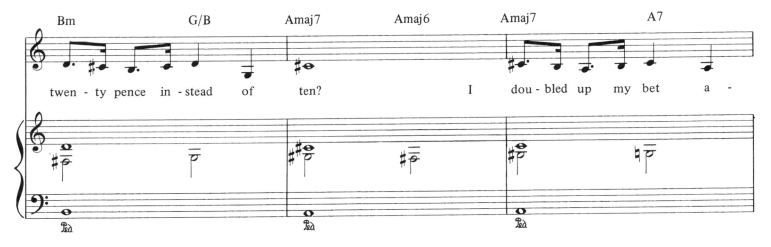

twen - ty pence in - stead of ten? I dou - bled up my bet a -

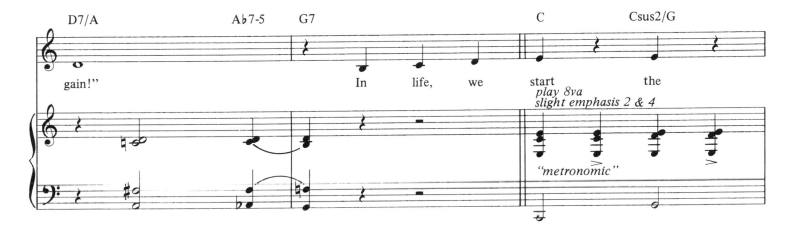

gain!" In life, we start the

play 8va
slight emphasis 2 & 4

"metronomic"

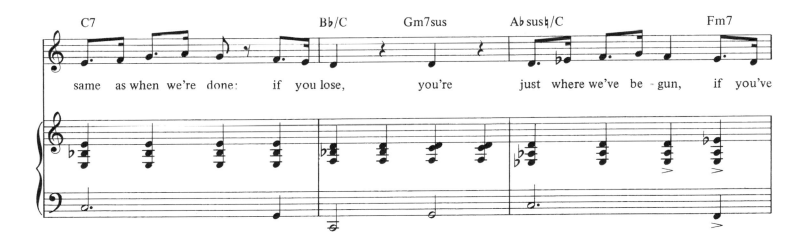

same as when we're done: if you lose, you're just where we've be - gun, if you've

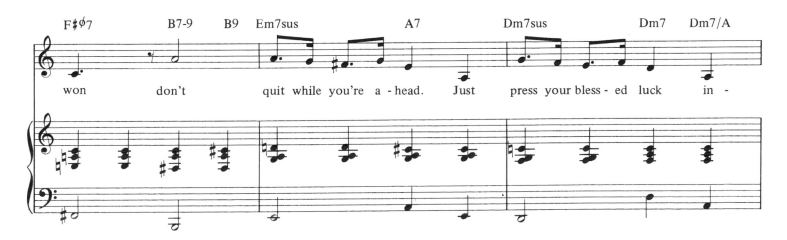

won don't quit while you're a - head. Just press your bless - ed luck in -

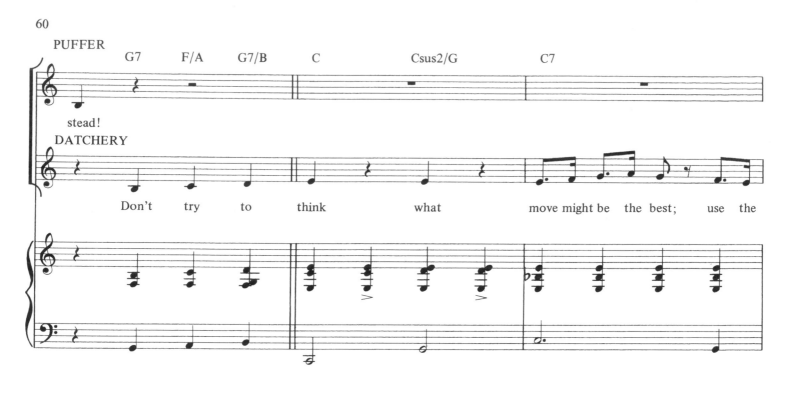

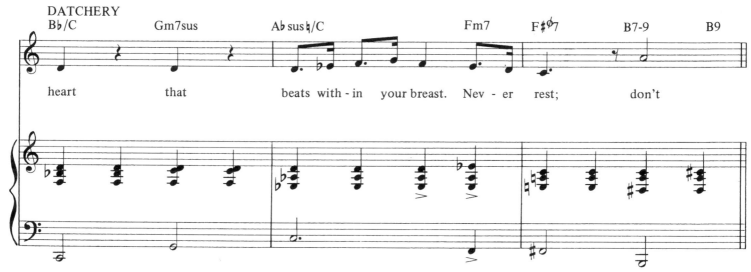

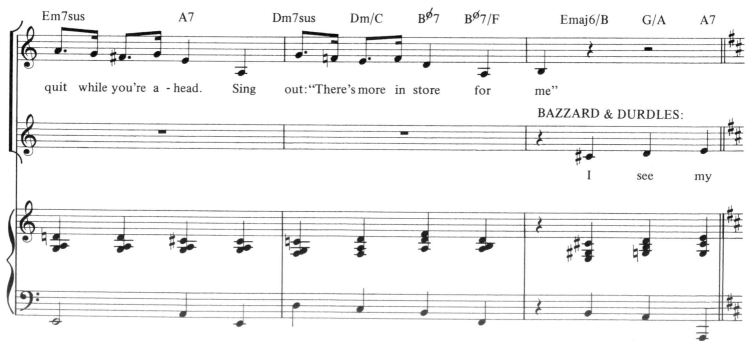

NEVILLE & CRISPARKLE:

wor - ry how you tread, Who cares? And there's (the) chance one

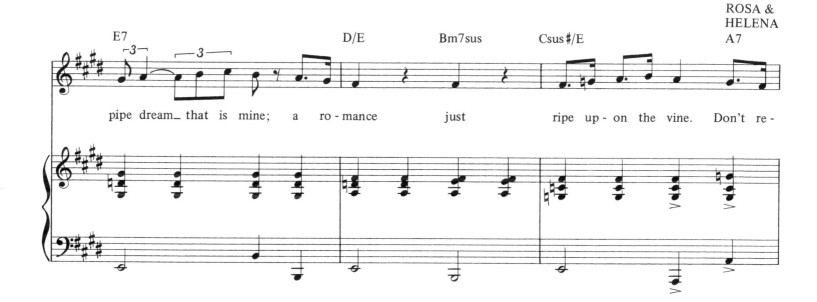

ROSA & HELENA

pipe dream_ that is mine; a ro - mance just ripe up - on the vine. Don't re -

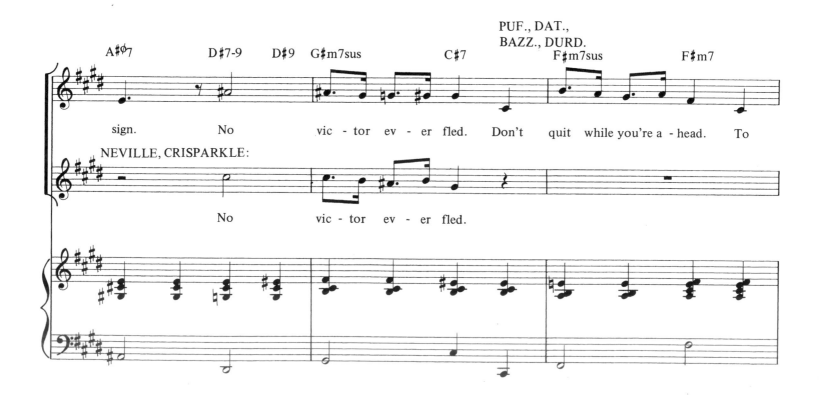

PUF., DAT., BAZZ., DURD.

sign. No vic - tor ev - er fled. Don't quit while you're a - head. To

NEVILLE, CRISPARKLE:

No vic - tor ev - er fled.

THE GARDEN PATH TO HELL

Words and Music by
RUPERT HOLMES

—Piano Accompaniment may be played an octave higher.—

Piano Accompaniment may be played an octave higher.

found my-self a wick-ed shelf where o-pi-um I sell. Here's a pipe for you, sir.

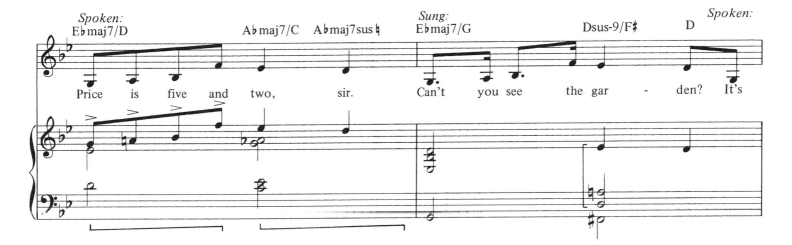

Spoken: Price is five and two, sir. *Sung:* Can't you see the gar - den? It's

such a love-ly gar - den. I'll take you there, I know the path so

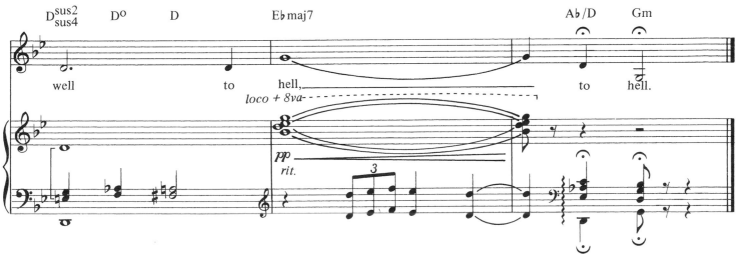

well to hell, to hell.

THE WRITING ON THE WALL

Words and Music by
RUPERT HOLMES

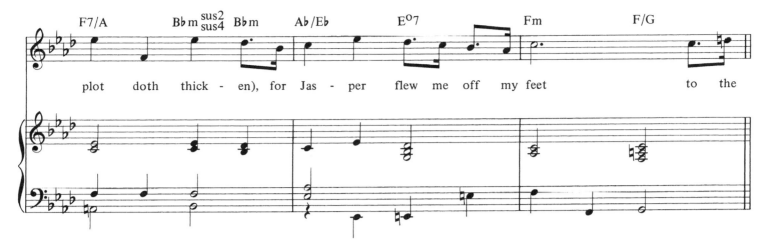

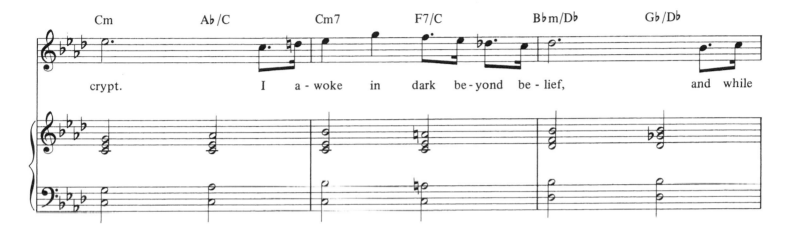

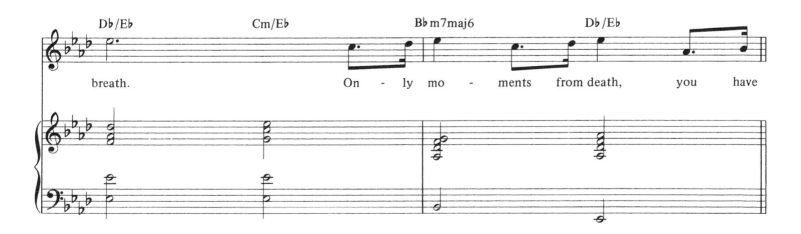

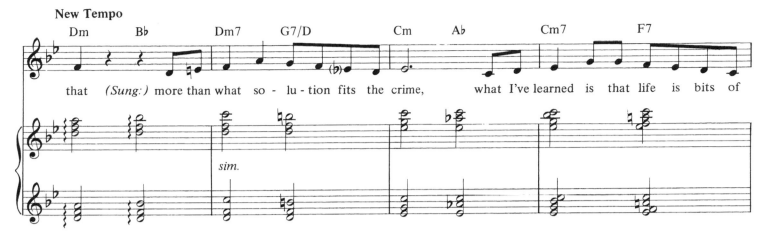

New Tempo

that *(Sung:)* more than what so - lu - tion fits the crime, what I've learned is that life is bits of

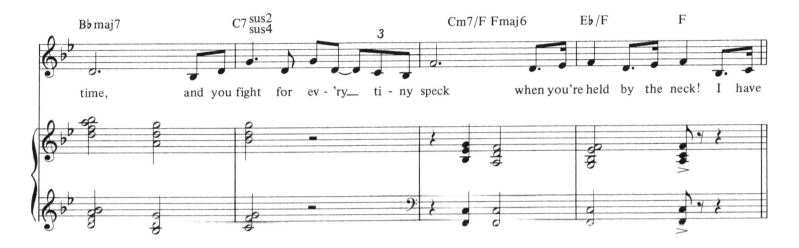

time, and you fight for ev - 'ry— ti - ny speck when you're held by the neck! I have

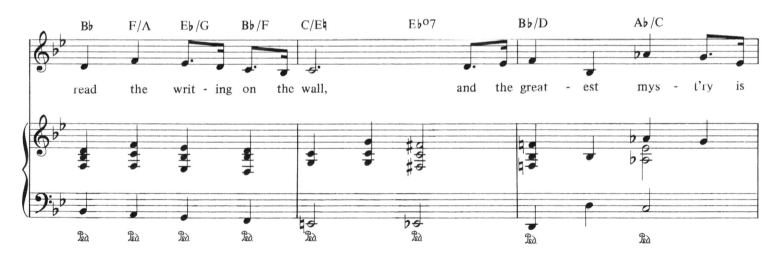

read the writ - ing on the wall, and the great - est mys - t'ry is

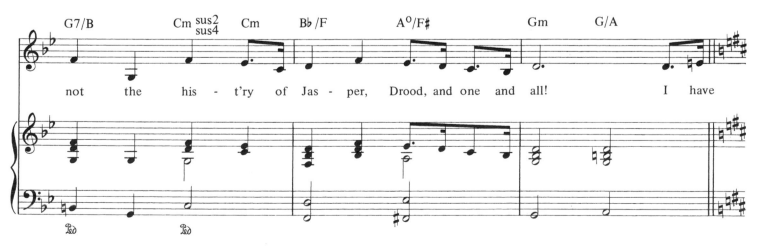

not the his - t'ry of Jas - per, Drood, and one and all! I have

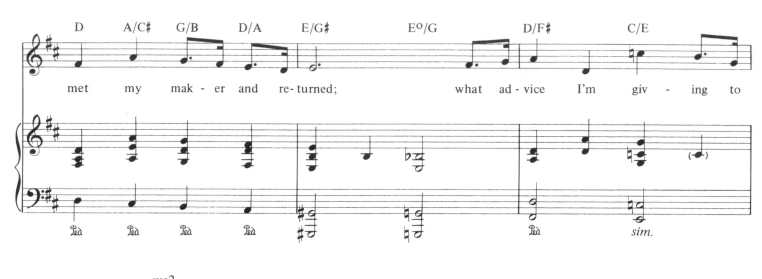

met my mak-er and re-turned; what ad-vice I'm giv-ing to

all those liv-ing is just to learn what I have learned. Life is dear. There can

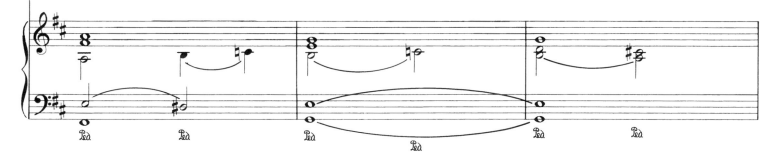

be no vic-t'ry in de-feat. If out-num-bered, beat a fast re-

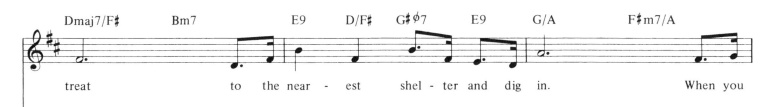

treat to the near-est shel-ter and dig in. When you

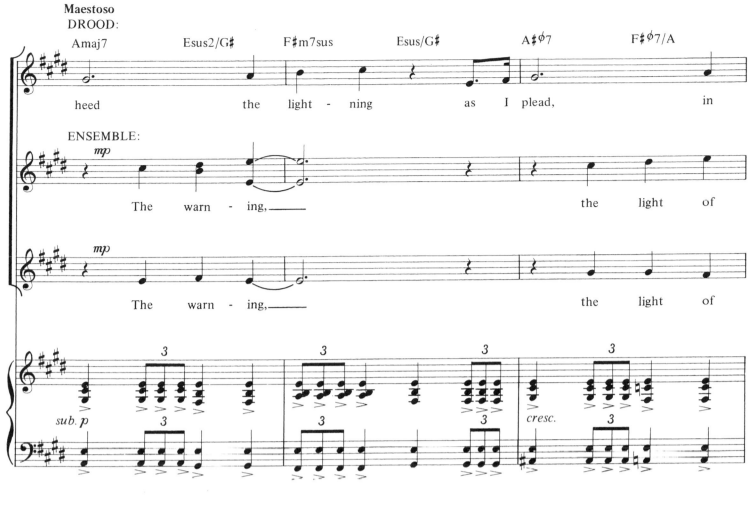

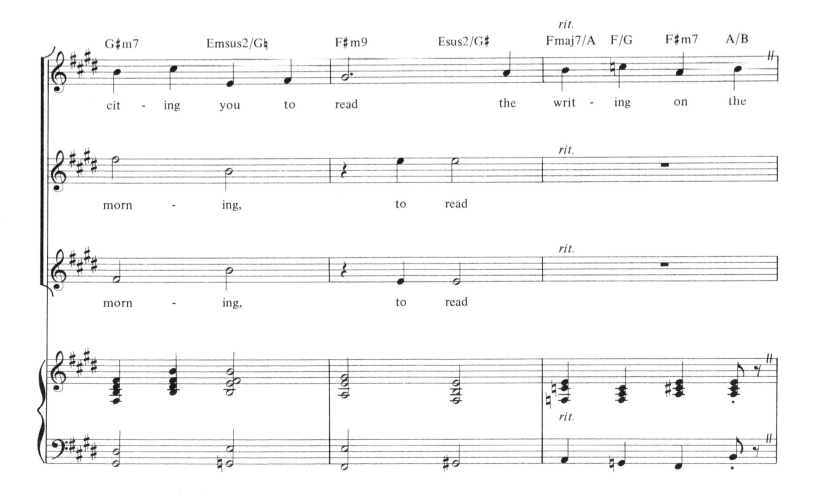